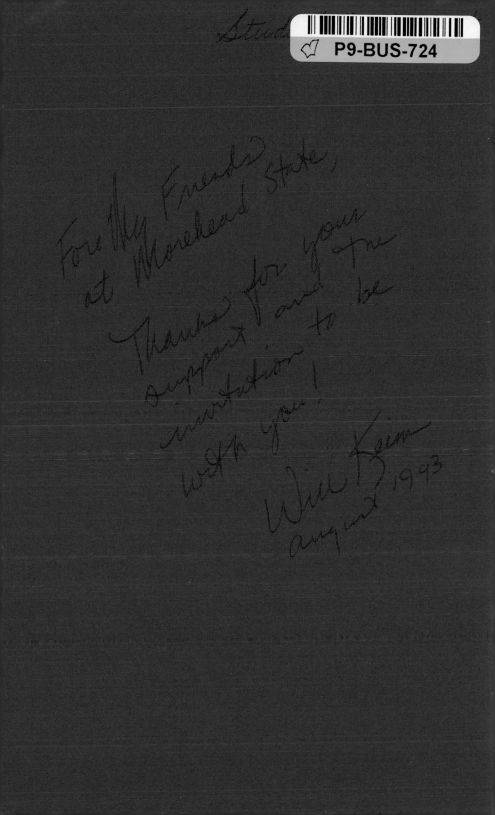

Stud...

For My Friends
at Morehead State,

Thanks for your
support and the
invitation to be
with you!

Will Keim
August 1993

A small book with a big and powerful message! Students can open it to ANY lesson on any day and find something that will inspire and teach them. Will Keim speaks from the heart to the heart.

Dr. Juliann Martinez
President & Educational Consultant
The Humor Connection
Granby, Massachusetts

I think it would be valuable for a college student to re-read this book every year and make diary-style notes, of their thoughts and progress in almost every section of the book.

Mike Kopetski
Member of United States Congress

As an employer, 1 look for candidates who embrace Keim's philosophy: *Love what you do and do it well.* Everything in one's career follows this concept.

Jon S. Saltzman
President
Penn-America Insurance Company
Pennsylvania

It's no accident that Will Keim is such a successful speaker. He has a message that is true and important and in this book he presents it in such a way that students will buy into it.

Mary Beth Seiler, Advisor
Panhellenic Association
University of Michigan

Drawing from great philosophers, current day contemporaries, and his own personal experiences, Will Keim presents many of the most critical lessons of life in a way that truly inspires the reader. *The Education of Character* is a complete and concise orientation, a gift of insights, attitudes and moral principles that, when embraced, empowers students to succeed.

Richard T. Hage
Dean of Student Affairs
Plymouth State College
New Hampshire

The Education Of Character: Lessons For Beginners is a crisp, right-to-the-point book that effectively addresses a variety of topics with which college students have to grapple. It is easy but thoughtful reading and highly recommended for today's college and university students.

Judith M. Chambers
Vice President for Student Life
University of the Pacific
California

THE EDUCATION OF
CHARACTER:
LESSONS
FOR BEGINNERS

32 Lessons
For College & University Students
On The Art Of Being A Person

Will Keim, Ph.D.

Library of Congress Catalog Card Number: 91-90761
ISBN: 0-9631834-0-0

Published in the United States of America by
VIATICUM PRESS
345 N.W. 31st Street
Corvallis, Oregon 97330

Contents

DEDICATION

This book is dedicated to my students all over the world. You have made my life more fulfilling than I ever dreamed it could be! Thank you for sharing, caring, hoping, acting, and loving. This is your time...let us work together to make the world a safer and more loving place for the children.

Thank you and God Bless You!

In love,

Will Keim, Ph.D.

ACKNOWLEDGMENTS

I would like to thank my family and express my love and appreciation to my wife, Donna, and daughters, Christa and Samantha who have all been very patient and supportive of me during the writing stages of this book.

Appreciation and gratitude are due to several colleagues and friends who have taken some of their precious and valuable time to critique the initial draft and provide suggestions for improvement. Their efforts have greatly improved the final product. They include:

Judy Chambers	Mary Beth Seiler
Dr. Craig Franz	Dr. Margaret Barr
Dean Richard Hage	Barbara Panzl
Greg LaFleur	Mrs. Bernstein
Jon Saltzman	Greg Hauser
Brad Ferguson	Dr. Frank Ragulsky

Special recognition is given to:

Dan Ahern	Dr. Juliann Martinez
Senator Mark Hatfield	Congressman Mike Kopetski
Josh Bernstein	Margaret Watkins
Ken Taylor	Dave Westol, J.D.
Dr. Ed Bryan	Dr. David Stephen

Finally, I wish to thank Tricia Lott for her invaluable assistance in the editing and production of the book. *The Education Of Character: Lessons For Beginners* would not have happened without her.

Will Keim

PREFACE

Becoming a person of character and integrity is more than knowing moral principles, laws, consequences, and motives. Becoming a person of character eventually includes having the COURAGE to act on what is right. Many people know what they should do...while far fewer people have the courage to act on their convictions. Becoming a person of character and integrity requires courage.

Life is precious and frequently undervalued. Each day is a gift. Not everyday will feel like a holiday, but each has its purpose and opportunity. Somedays will be full of challenge (overwhelming perhaps), others joy, and others learning. Sometimes giving to others and sometimes to ourselves. You may simply become a lot smarter by saying I'll never do that again. Life is a gift...don't waste it.

You are not bulletproof. You may believe that IT CAN'T HAPPEN TO ME...but IT CAN. Bad decisions about alcohol, drugs, sex, and speed can kill you. You may have had a friend who has died or has been permanently disabled. Your friend probably thought that IT would only happen to someone else...the day before. Life is what you have been given today. So much is wasted with the attitude that I'll do something <u>after</u> I graduate or <u>after</u> I get a job or <u>after</u> I get married or <u>when</u> I get into the real world. This is the real world...a unique time...but the <u>real</u> world. This is your life now. Treat it as a treasure.

Dr. Bruce M. Pitman,
Dean of Student Advisory Services
University of Idaho

xvii

FOREWARD

"We can do no great things - only small things with great love."   Mother Theresa

This is a very small book written with great love. Love for life, love of student, and love for the vitality and exuberance that students bring to everything they touch. It is a book about the education of character.

These are the lessons of my life. Life continues to amaze and instruct me daily. My father used to say,"If you're not careful, you'll learn something new everyday." Each day presents us with wonderful opportunities and challenges.

I wrote this book to help you understand the lessons that life is teaching you. The following pages will reveal the major challenges, problems, and possibilities you may encounter. Each lesson has been chosen carefully. Each word selected to help you find your way through the university experience and into life.

Thank you for including my thoughts in the education of your character. My life has come to me in lessons gleaned from experience, failure, and achievement. Your lessons will be unique, but we can learn from each other's triumphs and defeats..

Let the lessons begin!

Will Keim

THE
LESSONS

"Always do right. This will gratify some people and astonish the rest."

Mark Twain

LIFE

Life Is Not A Dress Rehearsal

"Life is what happens to you when you're making other plans."   Betty Talmadge

L ife is not a dress rehearsal. There are basically two ways to look at it. You may choose to be the director of your life or its victim. Your choice is made daily in each situation you encounter. No decision is more important, everything depends on it. Anaïs Nin said, "We don't see things as they are, we see them as we are."

There can be no doubt that we have all at times been victims. Situations have been thrust upon us that have hurt us, made us question things we previously believed in, and caused us pain. We cannot change the past but we can change the way we see the past. And we can learn from our disappointments. "Failure," wrote Henry Ford, "is only the opportunity to more intelligently begin again."

You are the director of your life play. You need not be its victim any longer. You have the lead in this play. You are in charge. You can choose to direct and star in your life story. Create the scenes. Direct the play! Yell, "cut," when you need a brief time-out. Enlist the assistance and talents of the best supporting actors and actresses you can assemble. Seek good counsel and listen well. No one can, nor will, direct the play for you because your story is an original.

Do not fly blindly into the light of self understanding as if a moth unsuspectingly approaching the candle flame. Go slowly...proceed with caution. Surround yourself with friends to support you when the inner journey becomes difficult. There is nothing inside yourself to be afraid of because you are good and you are worth your effort.

If you direct your life play then you stand a good chance of finding yourself. You may never be happy until you make your own choices and accept the consequences of them. Do not be afraid, for it has been my experience that wherever we go, we do not travel alone.

Seize the day. Climb the mountain. Direct your play. "Action!"

Remember:
- Life Is Not A Dress Rehearsal
- You Are The Director Of Your Life
- Seek Good Counsel. You Need Not Walk Alone.

PAIN

There Can Be Great Pain And Sadness In Life

"Life is pain, highness, and anyone who says differently is selling something." Wesley (The Dread Pirate Roberts) in the movie <u>The Princess Bride</u>, Director Rob Reiner

There can be great pain and sadness in life. I wonder at times how we carry on. Only the most sensational suffering merits headlines and news bytes, but we all suffer, we ache, we hurt, and God willing, we get through it. Life, for many, is pain full.

Yet, this book is about hope. It is about the goodness within each of us. It is about the power we have to change our lives and our perceptions of ourselves and others. I want to inspire, comfort, and heal. I want love and hope to jump off each page and into your heart.

But I didn't want to pretend there was no pain. Divorced parents, sexual abuses, problem drinking, eating disorders, drunk driving deaths, AIDS, financial instability...I know the pain, and so do you. But, I also know the Spirit. I have felt the healing touch. I am hopeful, for you, for me, and for our world. We can survive the pain. Grow because of it, together!

Eleanor Roosevelt advised, "You must do the thing you think you cannot do." We can cope with the pain if we learn to reach out to one another in hope and in love. We must, as Leo Buscaglia admonishes, "Choose the way of life..." and the way of life is love.

Understand:
- Everyone experiences pain and sadness in living.
- Your feelings are real. If it hurts bad, tell a friend or a counselor on campus.
- Love of yourself and others will "ease the pain" and give you hope. Choose the way of life!

PASSION

Be Present This Moment: Body, Mind, and Spirit

"Then from a remote part of his soul, from the past of his tired life, he heard a sound."   Herman Hesse in <u>Siddhartha</u>

There is a great voice within you that moves you toward persons, ideas, and things with great feeling, affect, and fervor. The voice stirs your heart, stimulates your mind, and calls you passionately into relationship with others. Are you too busy or unwilling to hear and feel the voice?

Are the sounds of modern life so loud that you cannot hear your inner voice? Do you feel tugged in so many directions that you cannot focus on what is most important to you? Would you like to feel the joy of pouring yourself totally into a project, an idea, or a cause?

There is one thing I would tell you if you would listen: Choose all you do with passion. Throw yourself into your life with disciplined abandon. Put your heart into your life and your body will follow. Be fully present this moment; physically, psychologically, and spiritually. Feel the joy of finishing a book read just for fun. Experience the indescribable pleasure of working with others on the completion of a common task. Relish the ecstasy of a grade won in all out effort.

St. Francis said, "Do few things and do them well." Most of the time we do many things just well enough. What do you do with passion? What do you love to do? Focus, plan, and discipline yourself. Pour yourself fully into your major, your residence hall, your weightlifting, your life. Feel the power of passion!

You cannot buy passion; it is not for sale. Drugs cannot induce it nor can they sustain it. Passion is not the same as sex, though sex can be with passion. Passion is purpose; the soul moving power that lies in each of you. Let it flow. Let it go. Watch it grow. No holding back. Use it to give life; to *your* self and to others. Be present this moment.

Do you feel that sensation in your heart right now, the excitement at the mere possibility of really feeling what I have described? That is but the tip of the iceberg of the power of passion. Passion for living is the gift you give yourself and there is no end to it!

Feel:
- The Power of Passion Within Yourself
- The Energy That Passion Creates In You
- The Reality That Your Life Is In Your Hands Now...Create It And Live It With Passion!

PURPOSE

The Secret Of College And University Life

"To love what you do and feel that it matters - how could anything be more fun?"   Katherine Graham, Publisher

When all is said and done, you are very likely to have spent at least half your waking life on your profession or vocation. What a tragedy it would be if you had spent so much time on something that meant so little to you.

The secret of college and university life is this: Find something you love to do and do it well enough that someone will pay you to do it.

I had the privilege of meeting Kevin Costner at a Delta Chi Fraternity meeting in the summer of 1990. We had a moment together and I had the opportunity to thank him for The Field of Dreams because it let me cry for an hour about my father's death. He thanked me. _Can you imagine?_ Kevin told the young men in attendance that someone would always be telling them what to do with their lives. "This is called conventional wisdom." "Sometimes," Kevin said, "those people are wrong." So follow your heart. What a beautiful testament

<u>Dances With Wolves</u> became to Kevin's advice to "follow your heart!"

Seek out those fields of endeavor, of study, of search and research, that fill your heart and mind with passion and your spirit with hope. In the end it really doesn't matter what others think is your best choice of major or vocation. What matters is this: "Can you live with your choices? Do your decisions excite your mind with endless possibilities and a feverish desire for the pursuit of your dreams?"

"The highest reward for a person's toil," wrote Ruskin, "is not what they get for it, but what they become by it." Your life will become a series of choices and the consequences of those choices. Choose wisely. Listen to the inner voice, and follow your heart with all the passion, focus, and discipline you can muster.

The rest-of-real-life outside of college will provide you with further training to do a specific job. Your employer will be looking for a person who loves to learn, is open to constructive feedback, and someone who is self initiating and motivated. You will discover and develop these qualities only in a major field that excites you.

<u>Promise Yourself:</u>
- I Will Trust My Feelings
- I Will Follow My Heart
- I Will Find Something I Love To Do And Do It Well Enough That Someone Will Pay Me To Do It

YOURSELF

The Real Struggle In College Is To Be Your Self

"Knowing others is intelligence; knowing yourself is true wisdom. Mastering others is strength; mastering yourself is true power."   Lao-Tzu

Life cannot be lived fully and authentically while you pretend to be someone that you are not or by attempting to find yourself by emulating others. You are not the unidimensional model on the cover of a four-color, high gloss magazine. They are posing for profit; you are living in reality.

We smile when we are hurting. Posing and posturing. We stand frozen with fear. Our spirit calls out for another human soul to comfort us. Yet we feel unable to move, concerned with what "they" will think. *This is not real.* Do you want to be yourself or pretend to be what others would pressure you to become?

The real struggle in college is to find and be yourself. If you stop "seeming" to be someone you are not, then you may "be" who you really are. What a tragedy it would be to go through college with an appearance reflecting but a dim image of the reality that is you.

Get to know yourself. There is no need to pretend to be someone you are not. Be yourself and you will be admired for being the rare person you are. Knowing yourself is true wisdom. Being yourself is true freedom. The day that you stop seeming to be someone you are not is the day when you will open yourself up to all the wonderful possibilities of being who you really are. That day can be today!

Consider:
- Being Real And Being Authentic
- Being Your Self By Reaching Out To Others
- Being Unafraid Of You. You Are Good And Love Able

EDUCATION

The Real Meaning Of Education

"Education worthy of the name is essentially the education of character."
                                                        Martin Buber

Here is the real story of life at the college and university level:

First you arrive. Then, the professors, student services professionals, staff, and students engage you in a series of potentially thought and growth producing episodes including, but not limited to, classes, seminars, labs, field study, extracurricular activities, parties, home football games, art shows, concerts, choir, performances, cultural events, for four to six years depending on your effort, time, and funding. At this time you leave the university as a more mature human being. Racially, culturally, educationally, socially, individually, and spiritually more sensitive, you depart to genuinely participate in the creation of human community and the betterment of the world in which you live. You then are ready to leave the world better than you found it; with a more peaceful appearance, just, and safe for the children. Your children, my children and the children of a billion people you have not met.

You spend a lifetime making ethical decisions, living in community, and developing a sense of purpose and self worth that assists others in discovering the goodness in themselves.

Simply put, the more involved you become in and out of class, the greater chance you stand of leaving the campus as a more educated person.

That is it. Education as I see it; education as you can choose to live it. You will additionally and inconsequentially have more personal stature in your community as an educated person, make your parents happy, make more money, and be a more attractive significant other. You may even use your education to purchase a Mercedes Benz. These are, however, by-products, at best, of higher education.

Your children will remember you for the kind of person you were. The insights you had, the love you shared. They will inherit, but not be touched by, your money, cars, and stock portfolio. As you leave this life your children will hold your hand, because you were smart enough to know what really mattered in life. Be smart. Be real. Be educated.

Education will prove to be the way to a better self and ultimately to a way of improving everything you touch. It is your most important investment in your self. The character you develop through education is truly your own!

Learn:
- That Education Worthy Of The Name Is Essentially The Education Of Character
- That The Really Important Outcome Of Higher Education Is What Kind Of Person You Become
- That While Education Is Expensive, The Price Of Ignorance Is Incalculable

FINANCES

Thoughts On Money, Credit, and Stress

"To the eyes of a miser a guinea is far more beautiful than the sun, and a bag worn with the use of money has more beautiful proportions than a vine filled with grapes. The tree which moves some to tears of joy is in the eyes of others only a green thing which stands in the way. As a man is, so he sees." Blake

O<u>n Money</u>...money is important only in as much as you must have some of it to house, clothe, and feed yourself. More of it increases luxury and puts more choices at your discretion. Money is not the meaning of life. Great quantities of it can bring corruption and greed. I would rather be wealthy and happy than poor and happy. It is not money that makes you happy because it is not material things or power over them which brings happiness. _It is you, your choices, and your attitudes._ Seek financial responsibility, even security, but please do not take refuge in your bank account. You need people, not coins. Dollars make terrible lovers.

On Credit...credit is a fact of life. As with all "facts of life", knowledge is power. Know thyself and thy spending habits. Be able to differentiate between your wants and your needs. Credit can assist you or derail you.

College students are bombarded with offers that sound too good to be true. If it sounds too good to be true, it is.

I spent the first twenty years of my life getting into debt and the last twenty years trying to get out of it! You will pay back your credit balance with generous interest and a pound or two of blood, sweat, tears, and stress. Ask yourself, "What is the impact of pay back?", before you buy.

Do yourself a favor:

1. Use cash as often as possible
2. Pay off your bill each month
3. Learn to say no the hundreds of businesses seeking your money before you have earned it

On Stress...when my wife and I argue, it is usually about money. Owing money creates pressure. Many of the things I thought I needed were actually nonessentials that I wanted. Student loans for tuition, books, fees, or rent are good investments. Credit expenditures for stereos or compact discs are poor investments. Invest in yourself. Be debt free or work toward it, and reduce stress.

Common Cents:
- Watch Your Pennies And Your Dollars Will Take Care Of Themselves.
- Spend Cash Whenever Possible.
- Pay Off Your Credit Balance Each Month.

CONSUMERISM

You Are The Consumer Of The Product Education

"Don't compromise yourself. You are all you've got ."
Betty Ford

You are more important than your college or university will sometimes make you feel. When you stand in line all day to register, add, or drop a class, it is hard to feel great about yourself and your use of time. If your personal identity has been reduced to a social security number you may begin to wonder who you really are. After you have colored in another "bubble exam" with a number 2 pencil only remembering to stay within the lines, you might justifiably question your true ability to express yourself.

The university exists as a "community of search" to preserve and transmit the culture and what is known to YOU the next generation of contributors, stewards, and leaders. You are the "reason for the season" of higher education; You are the consumer of the product education.

Do you receive good customer service at your school, or do they treat you better at the grocery store or corner bar? If you went to market and asked for a cut of beef and were told, "you will eat chicken you worthless life form"...would you stay and shop there? I would hope not. Why expect less from your university? The university or college that you attend does not exist to grant your every desire. But it ought to practice an "ethic of care" about you, making your needs an institutional priority.

Martin Buber believed, "Contact is the primary word in education." Yet we often put our least experienced instructors with our least experienced students. This is a recipe for educational disaster. It would seem to make more sense to put master teachers with the least experienced students.

The absolute and very least your institution should be able to give you is care. Care for your academic life, social life, basic needs of housing and food, and recreation. Caring for students is standard equipment, not an extra, or optional item. If your university does not care for you, let someone know. Your parents, the Dean, the student newspaper. If you are treated poorly, consider transferring to an institution of care. An institution that understands the importance of the customer and wants to provide quality educational services. If enough of you leave, then they will get the message. Unfortunately, money often speaks the loudest. You are the customer, spend your education dollar wisely.

Look for value returned on dollars spent. Identify professors and staff who are prepared and who care for you and lavish your class attendance and time on them. You are important, you matter, and the quality of your education will go a long way toward determining the quality of your life. Be in close "contact" with yourself and your educational institution. Expect the best from yourself and your university, then choose to make it happen.

I'm Saying:
- You Are The Consumer Of The Product Education
- Shop Wisely And Look For Good Service
- It Is Your Responsibility To Select "Quality Goods" From This Marketplace Of Education

PARENTS

Was Your Home Address In Heaven Or Hell?

"Are you capable of forgiving and loving the people around you, even if they have hurt you and let you down by not being perfect? Can you forgive them, and love them, because there aren't any perfect people around and because the penalty for not being able to love imperfect people is condemning oneself to loneliness?"
Rabbi Harold Kushner, When Bad Things Happen to Good People

If your parents' names are Ozzie and Harriett Nelson, Claire and Cliff Huxtable, or Ward and June Cleaver, then leaving home will be difficult because you will miss the love and caring of those parents, brothers and sisters, and friends.

If you lived on "Elm Street" or left an abusive situation, then you may be relieved to be leaving home, "getting away from it all." Or will you? Sally Kempton advises, "It is hard to fight an enemy that has outposts in your head."

If you are like most of us, you probably moved a lot as a child and lived physically and psychologically in places that were discomforting, disquieting or both. It is silly for us to believe that something is wrong with us because our families do not act like the television families.

19

Screen families always seem to be in the same residence and argue over things that never border on the real issues of life. Their families are an endless source of harmony and comfort. Our families have problems.

Two thoughts may comfort you. First, the people on television are just acting. Their shows are filmed in the land of fake-believe. Father didn't always know best, Donna Reed is dead, all African-American families are not parented by a doctor or lawyer, housed in a townhouse filled with love. Talking back to parents in real homes results in strained relations at best, not laugh track induced giggling. In real life, wisecracking children, youth, and adults abusing each other with doltish, moronish sarcasm is not funny. To use "Roseanne" or "The Simpsons" as family-relations training videos is to make a dreadful mistake.

Second, most of your parents did the best they were capable of doing. Some parents chose to do less. A few were abusive, some negligent, but all at worst provided you with life and the possibility of a better future. You have either learned how to be a good parent or seen how not to raise a child. It is time to move forward, some with joy, many with pain. But all alive with hope.

This is your life now and leaving home has made it possible to move on to a more independent state. Perhaps the greatest African-American baseball pitcher of all time, Satchell Paige, once said, "Never look back, someone might be gaining on you!" I say *never* look back because you cannot change a thing except for those adjustments you make today. You must learn from your past so that you are not condemned to repeat it. But after that, look to today. This is your day: Seize the day!

Recall:
- Most People Around You Share Your Pain Of Growing Up And Leaving Home
- Your Past Is A Teacher: Learn From It
- Life Is Not A Television Sit-Com: Your Life Is Real And Is Your Creation

FRESHMAN

A Growing Person Is Always A Freshman
(At Something)

"I tried and failed. I tried again and succeeded."
Gail Borden, Jr.

If you are growing as a passionate and authentic human being, then you are always a freshman at something. My mentor and master professor Dr. Don Duns told me this in 1971. This is because you are always learning or trying something new. You are not afraid to say, "I do not know," nor are you afraid to fail. Life constantly presents you with opportunities to learn or try something new. Being a freshman or being new means you are entitled to not know everything.

I am a "freshman" at golf...fifty yard drives, condo-battering slices, and five putt greens. You simply cannot look more bewildered and uncertain as a college or university freshman than I do on a golf course. I will be a "senior" in golf one day and you will be doing better on campus.

Let's have a little patience, shall we? After all, we survived high school and it is nearly impossible to be more out-of-it than a high school freshman, isn't it? Then again, you have never seen me golf. Have courage. You are making progress.

We must be willing to take some risks. Fear of failure debilitates us. Erica Jong said, "The trouble is, if you don't risk anything, you risk even more." Failure is only temporary, a brief stop on the way to success.

One wise and wealthy businessman told me on a flight going into the Los Angeles International Airport, "I do not ask the students I hire out of college to tell me about their successes. Rather I ask them to describe to me their biggest failures. I learn more about them in the five minutes after that question than in all successes listed in their resumes."

If they have not failed, then he suspects that they have never put their goal beyond their grasp.

If they failed because of the incompetencies of those around them, then he expects how the student will one day feel about him.

But if the student describes his or her plan, what went wrong and accepts some responsibility for the outcome, then that student becomes a potential employee.

Be proud that you have again begun a new path of growth. Your journey, though frightening, will be a great one. "You grow up," writes Edith Barrymore, "the day you have your first real laugh - at yourself." Lighten up a bit. Things are going to be all right.

Freshman And New Students:
- Be Proud: You Are Making Progress
- Be Open To New Experiences: Don't Be Afraid To Fail
- Be Aware That Everyone Is A Freshman At Something

EXPERIENCE

Your College Friends May Not Laugh At Your High School Jokes

"A difference of taste in jokes is a great strain on the affections."
George Eliott

Be clear that your high school friends laughed at your jokes because they liked you. They grew up with you and knew you, played sports with you, hung out with you, and became conditioned to find you amusing. However, this is college. Give your new friends and roommates at college time to appreciate the fullness of your humor.

This is called experience. It is also called transition; that is, making the move from one stage of your life to another. Adolescence to adulthood. High school to college. Transitions occur between important stages of one's life and often produce stress. Each day in life, each event, provides us with the opportunity to change and grow. Holding on to old patterns of coping in new situations causes us to get out of step with the realities of our new home. Experience teaches us that growth is sometimes painful but always necessary for real life. "Experience," said Aldous Huxley, "is not what happens to a man. It's what a man does with what happens to him."

It might not hurt to develop some new material as well. Really, you were tired of the old predictable patterns of things in high school anyway. The same old classes, the same old clubs. You were ready for something new. Weren't you? Onward! Upward! You know you really do not want to go back. And besides, you can't. Open yourself up to the wonders of life at the university. See the possibilities. Take the first step toward the experience of a lifetime.

A Final Word To The Wise

Many wise and experienced people did not attend college. They have graduated from the School of Hard Knocks with a Ph.D. in Life. You would be wise to let them teach you what they have learned through their experience. There is no better teacher than experience.

Recognize:
- Growth Comes With Experience And Transitions
- Experience Is Sometimes Painful And/Or Anxiety Producing
- Let Other People's Experience Teach You

ATTENDANCE

Class Is A Lot Like Life: You Will Do Better If You Show Up

"No matter how much time you wasted in the past, you still have an entire tomorrow. Success depends upon using it wisely by planning and setting priorities." Denis Waitley,
The Joy of Working

Attendance at most colleges and universities is voluntary. Roll is not taken in many places. And so it is in Life. Students who choose not to show up for classes establish a pattern that unfortunately trains them and teaches them a negative approach to life. This, believe me, will severely limit your chances of success and the enjoyment your education might bring you.

When you go to class every day you:

1. Keep in touch with changes in the course syllabus.
2. Get better return on your tuition dollar investment.
3. Put your face with your name which assists the professor in grading a human being rather than a social security number.

Much of success hinges on being present when important decisions are made and important topics are discussed. Knowledge is power. Feeling power<u>ful</u> minimizes feeling power<u>less</u>. Simply put, if you go to class, not only will your G.P.A. be higher, but so will your sense of self. I know you want to do well, and feel good about yourself. I know you can if you will help yourself by showing up for class and your life. Woody Allen said, "Most of success in life is showing up." Call your own roll. Don't be absent from your life. Life is one "class" you get to take only once. Ace it!

Strive To:
- Attend Every Class Every Day
- Be Present Physically And Psychologically
- Show Up For Class (And Life): You'll Do Better

STUDYING

How To Be A Good Student

*"Quality is never an accident; it is always the result of high
intention, sincere effort, intelligent direction, and skillful
execution; it represents the wise choice of many alternatives."*
Willa F. Foster

Maximize The Missing Minutes (M+MMs©). This
approach advocates that you study during the
day between classes instead of shooting pool or watching
the Soaps on television. You can usually pick up 2-4
hours of quality daytime studying and eliminate a good
portion of your homework.

With a saddening acceptance of mediocre performance
on all levels of our society and your need to "fit-in"
and be accepted, this sudden academic surge may make
you stick out, raise your G.P.A. to threateningly high
levels, label you bookish, and perch the crown of
nerddom upon your head. That would assume, of course,
that you saw someone you know in the library, which is
doubtful. While you are studying most of your friends
will be wondering who is going to be seduced next on
which show, how that character or this one came back
from the dead, or how everyone's life in daytime drama
can be so messed up.

After completing your secret daytime study you may then return to your residence hall, fraternity or sorority house and say, "Homework? Not tonight. I've got places to go, things to do, people to meet. See you!" Your friends will marvel. "How does he do it?" or, "I wish I had her attitude." "He's really get it together!" "She's cool."

Remember that uninformed "cool" people don't get jobs or into grad school. It ultimately is cool to study. Your job is to be the best student you can be. This will assist you in becoming your best professionally. You need to do your best. Doing your best, as Wilford Brimley puts it about eating oatmeal, is "The Right Thing To Do." Besides, in five years the people who "tease" you for being a good student will be going to get your coffee for you. Education is expensive and time consuming, but it's really cheap and a joy compared to a lifetime of ignorance and unfulfilled potential. Anne Frank believed, "Laziness may appear attractive, but work gives satisfaction." Give it a try!

Study:
- During The Day
- Between Classes
- Remembering Your M&MMs©

MAJOR

Choosing An Academic Discipline

"I have never let my schooling get in the way of my education."   Mark Twain

Your major course of study is only the <u>vehicle</u> that you drive on your journey through college, onto the freeway of character development, finally exiting onto the path <u>after</u> college — <u>real life</u>.

Depending on what plan you choose and how seriously you apply yourself, it will take you anywhere from 4 to 6+ years to get to your real life road — hopefully the one "less traveled," for this has proven to contribute significantly to the development of character, creativity, and the betterment of society.

Not everyone understands this! It was, however, Albert Einstein, who proposed, "Great spirits have always encountered violent opposition from mediocre minds." Mr. Einstein was thought to be quite intellectually challenged in his youth, perhaps even dyslexic. He had a different vision. He knew that choices were relative and that each person must choose and accept at times violent opposition from mediocre, or different, minds.

There is no set formula for selecting a major. However, I will suggest one way of choosing your field of study. You may choose to take the university or college catalog and a piece of paper. List all the courses that you are interested in and that you think would be fun. Lay them out in a four year period. Figure out what major you qualify for with the least amount of extra courses. This is your major! Nearly everyone will try to "help" you select your academic discipline. Not all the advice will be valuable. "Don't go into education, be a dentist." Five years later, the dental schools are closing because fluoride works, and one could have been credentialed to fill the teacher void created by trend-reactive major selection.

Study something you love. Something that really calls you into your books, the library, and into dialogue with your professors. What is important anyway at the end of it all is not only what you know, but who you know, and what kind of person you have become. After all, Ph.D.s are annually awarded for dissertations about: Science Fiction, Fantasy, Mystery Writers, Quantum Physics, The Influence of Rock'n'Roll, and Horror Films to name but a few. Study something you love that teaches you something about yourself.

As to "who you know"...the most important "connection" you need to make in college is with yourself. You will be pleasantly surprised by the person you discover within if you can forgive yourself, learn to trust yourself, give others the benefit of the doubt, and love yourself for the individual you are. Others would love you too if you would let them. But first you have to make contact with yourself and begin to develop your character.

Your major should help you do this. Otherwise it is a waste of your precious time and resources. My liberal arts bias tells me that your major and eventually your profession will be an extension of who you see yourself to be. I am an educator. It is who I am, who I see myself to be. What do you envision yourself doing? Who do you dream of yourself becoming? Walt Disney said, "All our dreams can come true if we have the courage to pursue them." Choose a major that gets you closer to your dream. Have courage. I believe you can reach your dream and find your self. Now I am asking you to believe it. Besides, the average student changes his or her major over 3 times. Be patient with yourself.

Choose:
- A Major That You Love
- A Major That Helps You Discover Yourself
- A Major Whose Professors Are The Kind Of Women And Men You Aspire To Be Like When Your Children Look Up To You

STRESS

Dr. Keim's Prescription For Stress Reduction

"You cannot shake hands with a clenched fist."
Indira Gandhi

You should know and believe that stress is normal. All persons experience stress in differing degrees. Stress can become debilitating. You can do some things to reduce or manage stress in your life.

I have found my life's stressful situations to be more manageable if I:

1. Sleep 6-8 hours each night.
2. Eat breakfast every day.
3. Take an IB4U hour daily.

> Translated: For 1 hour a day,
> **I** (my needs) come
> **B4** (before)
> **U** (your needs)

I am not advocating campus-wide selfishness. You cannot be of service to others if you do not service *your* self. I take ½ hour a day (at least) to sweat, i.e. weightlifting, stairmaster, life cycle, etc., followed by a ½ hour "down" time (which is really "up" time) of thought, contemplation, and/or prayer. Ask the soul searching questions of your existence after exercising and your mind will amaze you with its clarity. The insights you receive will be just like the taste of ice cold water from a crystal clear glass. A sip of the psyche for the quenching of the soul.

4. Make a "to do" list every night just before you go to bed and update it in the morning with things your peaceful rest reveals to you during your night's sleep.

5. Buy and use a weekly, monthly and yearly planner. List at the beginning of each term all the assignments for the whole term. Your professors should provide you with the term's assignments. If not, request one and then create a master list of all the term's requirements. Post it above your desk and check it often.

6. Do your M+MMs© (see Lesson 13) daily! And study on weekends! Another great time to grab a couple of extra hours is immediately following a light dinner.

7. Don't be afraid to go for help if the pressure becomes too heavy. People who talk to counselors are healthy people who will often gain new insights into the issues facing them. Campus life, especially for new students, creates pressure and stress builds up. It is normal, natural, and quite common to feel pushed and pulled from many directions.

Steps 1-6 will help you to reduce the pressure. It is not that stress is uniformly negative. Some stress can be positive. Stress can motivate you to get busy and accomplish your goals and objectives. My method is geared toward helping you eliminate excess stress. It works for me and I hope it will work for you. Step 7 provides a pressure release valve that is much healthier than alcohol or drugs. Burnout is real and demands professional care. You can find an attentive ear and a trained professional ear in the counseling office, Student Services, or related department. Most faculty members will make time for you as well, if you ask them. Give it a try.

I Am Telling You That:
- Stress Is Normal
- You Can Reduce Stress If You Try
- Help Is Available On Campus And The Nearby Community If You Need It.

ALCOHOL

If You Have Problems When You Drink
Then You Are A Problem Drinker

"It has been said that whenever you mention alcohol in our society people either get mad or thirsty." Philip L. Hansen, The Afflicted and The Affected

I t is okay not to drink.

Many students do drink alcohol. Many students have a great time and do not drink alcohol. As a matter of fact, very few students desire to or succeed in drinking to the point of inebriation without some peer pressure. I believe it is wrong to put pressure on persons to drink beyond their ability to control themselves. It is disrespectful and unfriendly. I want you to rise above this coercion. _It is okay not to drink._ You are an adult and I believe you can make informed choices about alcohol. I really do!

Many students do choose to drink. This is okay too. Especially when no laws are violated, the student practices responsible consumption, and low or no risk drinking results in healthy activity rather than hurtful behaviors.

There is a definition I would like you to think about. _If you have problems when you drink then you are a problem drinker._ What happens when you drink? Good things?

Positive social interaction? Self esteem-building behavior? Or drinking games that are not social lubricants but preludes to passing out? Life threatening driving episodes and sexual encounters? Health or hurling? You tell me! I am not trying to preach to you. I drink alcohol myself. But I do want you and I to be alive, healthy, and productive. Be honest with yourself.

Alcohol abuse is related to:

- Two-thirds all acquaintance rapes on campus
- Over a third of all student suicides
- 20,000 deaths a year on the highways
- Nearly two-thirds of all mental cruelty divorce cases
- Over half of the reasons students do not graduate from college.

Please make good choices...

North Carolina State University's The Alcohol Book says it quite nicely, "A very important part of college life is socializing. If all of your social life revolves around alcohol, you are using it as a crutch for social skills. Life can be enjoyable if you look beyond a passive crutch and get involved in the surrounding communities activities."

Need help? Want some more information? Check out your campus' BACCHUS Program, GAMMA group, SADD organization, AA/ACOA/AlAnon meetings, counseling office, or Dean of Students. What do all those letters mean? If you need help you'll find out. We have to help others help us by helping ourselves. There are students and staff on your campus ready to help you learn to manage your alcohol consumption. Are you ready to learn? A great number of students who do not get through the university fail to do so due to problem drinking by themselves or their parents. Do all you can to make sure this does not happen to you.

Some Final Thoughts About Drinking
- It's Okay Not To Drink. As A Matter Of Fact, For Students Under 21, It's Also "Legal" Not To Drink
- If You Have Problems When You Drink, Then You Are A Problem Drinker
- If You Choose To Drink, Please Do So In Moderation And In A "Low Risk" Manner, i.e. Don't Drink While Taking Medication, Driving, While You're Under Stress, Tired, Sick Or Likely To Put Yourself In A Compromising Situation. Make Moderation, Not Excess, Your Path!

DRUGS

How To Be Part Of The Solution, Not The Problem

*"Problems that remain persistently unsolvable should
always be suspected as questions asked in the wrong way."*
Alan Watts, The Book: On the Taboo of Knowing Who You Are

It strikes me as odd that our nation would spend so much time and money to destroy coca fields in other nations and conduct air and ground searches for marijuana fields when the real question perhaps is: *Why do so many people feel they need to live their lives in an altered state of consciousness?*

The war on drugs has focused primarily on the supply side of the issue. This is certainly a concern. The unbridled flow of narcotic substances from one nation to another is very serious. I want you to begin thinking about the demand side of the equation. Especially and primarily your demand.

Are public service announcements the best we can do to prevent drug abuse? It seems to me that we are either part of the solution to the drug problem or part of that problem. When we use drugs, we become the drug problem. Worse yet, we provide the same drugs we use to children. How?

43

When a gram, brick, or lid is purchased, it comes in a much larger quantity. Your lid adjoins another lid that now can be distributed to a high school student. Your demand supplies him. A gram in your hands places the same drug in the hands of an eighth grade young woman. She cannot handle it, even though you think you can. We must stop fooling ourselves. Honesty demands that we admit that if we are using, we are handing drugs to our own little brothers and sisters and other children we have not met. You might argue that you have a right to destroy your own life. Do you have a right to destroy your younger sister's life?

Students sometimes tell me, "Will, marijuana is just the same as alcohol." I tell them, "Really, when was the last time you saw someone who wasn't stoned eat a five pound block of cheese?" Granted, the media over-dramatizes the typical user of marijuana. *Reefer Madness* is before most of your times, but it is a classic portrait of how ignorant we have been in educating people about the real problems of drug use. To be honest, if I had to "legalize" alcohol or marijuana I would have to stop and think. When you pull over a stoner who is driving, the car is usually going 9 miles per hour. When you ask someone who is high in the Residence Hall to turn down his Pink Floyd, he laughs and accommodates you. Drivers under the influence and alcohol focused partiers are much more abusive. But it isn't up to me is it?

The fact, though, is that marijuana and other drugs are not the same as alcohol in the eyes of the state and federal government. Try this: Check the box marked "Have you been convicted of a misdemeanor or felony?" ❒ YES and call me when you get your next job interview. If you do not like the laws, then vote to change them. I will guarantee you that Medical School, Law School, Security Clearance Agents, or the Military will not reason with you that marijuana is the same as alcohol. Beware and be warned. Your future should not be negatively impacted because of substance use or abuse.

The bottom line is this. Drugs are illegal and hurtful to the progress of society and the betterment of the individual. At the same time our society spent fifty-nine billion dollars on alcohol last year, imported one hundred and fifty metric tons of cocaine, and established marijuana as the largest cash crop in several states. Our society is clearly in crisis between what we say and what we do regarding drugs. Your future may be negatively impacted by drug use. Your personal wellness will almost certainly be.

Here is a two step plan to being part of the solution:

1. Do not use. Stop or do not start.
2. Persuade your friends not to use.
   Persuade them by example.

Remember, if you use drugs you are handing them to children. I believe you are better than that. Now you believe it! We must overcome our national sedation and face our problems clear headed. Address the drug problem by eliminating the demand...your demand. It is the law of supply and demand. If you need the supply, then they can demand whatever they want from you. No demand by you...no supply by them. You win! And so does our nation and the world. Most importantly, **The children win...the children live!**

God bless the children and God bless you for not using. "Blessed are those that take care of the little ones," the Good Book says. Be well.

Think, Clear-Headed:
- I Can Live Drug Free
- Using Drugs Gives Drugs To Children
- I Will Be Part Of The Solution, Not The Problem, To The War On Drugs (even if I have to get help to quit using).

Lesson 18

SEX

The S.A.D. Connection Between Collegiate Sexuality, Alcohol and Drugs

"No problem can stand the assault of sustained thinking."
Voltaire

There was a time when sex was thought by many folks to belong in the bounds of marriage. While this may still be true in some communities, the campus environment seems to view sex as a rite of passage into adulthood. But is it? Now sex can kill you.

Certainly sex between consenting adults can be an exhilarating and life giving experience. Students have told me, "It makes me feel alive." "It makes me feel loved." "It felt great." Not all reports, however, have been so compelling and positive.

A recent *New York Times* article stated the United States was experiencing a 40 year high in the Sexually Transmitted Disease (S.T.D.) rates. Young men and women 15-24 led the way. A University of Virginia study contended that two out of every one thousand college students tested positive for AIDS (Acquired Immune Deficiency Syndrome) and that, in another UVA study, 38% of "regrettable sexual encounters" were

47

directly related to alcohol. At the time of this writing, The Center for Disease Control in Atlanta estimates there are currently over one and a half million AIDS carriers with over 200,000 dead in America due to AIDS. Incidentally, over 100,000 abortions a year are performed in the United States. There is clearly a sex, alcohol, and drug connection in our nation. Simply put, the more we drink, the higher we get, the poorer our decision making process in the area of sex becomes.

What to do?

> I propose **"Four Options For Sexual Responsibility In The '90s."** Choose wisely. Your life depends on it.

The Four Options:

1. Abstain. This is a nearly sure-fire way to avoid sexually transmitted diseases, AIDS, unwanted pregnancy, and "regrettable sexual experiences." Magic Johnson has spoken quite eloquently recently on the outcomes of sleeping around. His life will likely end prematurely because he did not abstain or practice safer sex. What a great loss. What a senseless tragedy. Magic is very brave to be so open about his situation. He is not a hero for "accommodating as many women as possible." His "accommodations" will likely kill him.

Let's be honest. Not everyone who is talking about sex is having it. I know because I talked about sex a lot during college. Allowing peer (or beer) pressure to coerce you into doing something you don't want to do gives someone else control over you. I know you do not want that.

48

Besides, while you are out practicing with someone else's future wife or husband, somebody is possibly practicing with the mother or father of your children. If you are honest I think you will admit that the idea of sharing your honeymoon bed with a "real experienced" partner isn't your optimal situation. If sex is an ultimate human experience, it strikes me that it should fit somewhere in a loving relationship, between two consenting, caring adults. For some this is called marriage. For you, it may be a serious premarital relationship. I would prefer that you waited or abstained. But you may not. I hope you do for your sake, your self-esteem, and for your future significant other.

But if you don't wait...if you choose to have sex... then please:

Practice Options 2, 3, and 4:

2. **Use a condom,**

3. **Use a condom,**

4. **Use a condom.**

"Using condoms is so embarrassing." Try explaining herpes on your wedding night for the true meaning of embarrassing. "Condoms ruin the spontaneity of sex." Who said sex is spontaneous? Unfortunately, probably many of the 200,000 dead AIDS victims. Sex was very spontaneous and deadly for them. My wife and I plan sex and it's kind of exciting! Please don't let Hollywood movies dictate your social or ethical mores. Many of the actors, directors, and producers live lives that are not compelling documentaries on responsible living.

And please, **Don't Die of Embarrassment**. Since the AIDS virus can lie dormant 5-7 years (maybe more), you are in effect sleeping with everyone your lover has slept with in the last 5-7 years. How well do you know him or her? You can get pregnant "doing it" only once, and even great (and protected) sex has powerful emotional, physical, and spiritual impact on you. Are you really ready? Be sure. Your life depends on it. I want you _alive_ and feeling good about yourself. It is all right _not_ to have sex. Anyone who uses guilt or alcohol and drugs to get you to have sex does not love you. Be clear.

First, respect yourself. Others will find it easier to respect you when you respect yourself. Second, respect others. Mistakes made in the past are just that...the past. Learn from them and make them no more. You have the potential, the power, and the possibility to change.

Finally, a parting thought. *Virginity is not a curse.* You can always decide to have safer sex. But you cannot decide to be a virgin again. Experience is a great teacher, but when it comes to sex in the '90's, experience can kill you. Be careful and be well. Your life is a precious gift. You have a unique contribution to make. I want you alive to make it!

Think Before You Have Sex:
- It Is Okay Not To Have Sex, Not Everyone Is Doing "The Wild Thing"
- Sex Is Never Safe, Only Safer
- Don't Die Of Embarrassment: Take Care Of Yourself

DATING

The Lost Art Of Dating

"Just remember, we're all in this alone."   Lily Tomlin

When you stop and think about it, most of the time what you really enjoy is time spent with another person. Time alone is necessary for mental health and at times peaceful, but only because it takes place in the context of on-going relationships, both romantic and non-romantic.

I think dating is a lost art. It has been replaced by dances, often times with wolves. We put the music on at volume level ten, drink to sedate ourselves, and look for someone to be with. Why is it that when students are single they want to act married, and when they are married they want to act single? Such a mystery is life. Perhaps a way to cope with loneliness is to resurrect the lost art of dating.

Good dating does not have to lead to immediate mating. At the risk of sounding like Bob Seger, "I wish I didn't know now what I didn't know then." But I do know some things now that I did not know then. There are few suggestions I would like you to think about before your next close encounter.

51

TEN DATING TIPS

1. Date a lot of different people.

2. Quit trying to find the "right one" and let the "magic one" sneak up on you.

3. Be sober on dates, leaving the "beer goggles" at home.

4. Talk to your date about your date's major, hometown, life in general.

5. Listen actively to your date.

6. Go out for food more on dates; what's a little pasta on your shirt? I know now I would have lived with a few spills.

7. Go to music programs more on dates; music brings people together.

8. Realize the Pointer Sisters weren't lying: take "slow hands" with you on dates.

9. Be assertive and direct...your date will respect you.

10. Know that since two-thirds of all collegiate rapes happen on dates and that alcohol is almost universally involved in this horrible act of violence,:
    A. Be sober
    B. Communicate your desires clearly
    C. "Say no/accept no" not as rejection but simply as "no"

Dating is not obligatory foreplay to sexual intercourse.

Dating is the art of spending time with someone, sharing and listening, and engaging a moment of time together. If it leads to a further relationship, great! If not, done properly, it still beats being alone.

If you read a lot, listen well, and care, you will be an enjoyable date. As to the idea that there is something wrong with the relationship if you/he/she sees other people: Get real. If someone else finds your date interesting you should be happy and see this as validation that you were right. Your date is worth spending time with. Jealousy reveals a low self-esteem, nagging self-doubt about whether you can stand up to the competition.

Dating can also occur in groups. If you are not asked out or fear rejection if you do the asking, grab a group of people and do something en masse. One of my favorite memories from the residence hall was of eight or ten of us being bored together. Loneliness was replaced by laughter and fear turned into friendships. Confucius said, "Our greatest glory is not in never falling, but in rising every time we fall." So get up and get busy making friends. You can make friends only by being one.

When Dating:
• See Interesting People
• Be An Interested Person
• Be Single When You're Single And Married When You're Married...Enjoy Yourself...Dating Is Supposed To Be Fun

WELLNESS

If You Are Healthy, Then You Are Wealthy: Ride The Cycle Of Life

"Life is not a 'brief' candle. It is a splendid torch that I want to make burn as brightly as possible before handing it on to future generations."　　　　George Bernard Shaw

I think of being well or healthy, as a three part process to the third power. It is a cycle of three primary concerns each within three areas of focus. The processes are **Exercise**, **Nourishment**, and **Rest**; the power comes from the **Mind, Body**, and **Spirit**. An outline may help you get the picture.

I. Exercise
   A. Mind - Read your textbooks
   B. Body - Half hour daily physical exercise
   C. Spirit - Half hour daily contemplation/prayer

II. **Nourishment**
   A. Mind - Read one newspaper daily, two magazines per week, one book monthly (for pleasure)
   B. Body - Eat breakfast daily and a balanced diet
   C. Spirit - Belong to a spiritual fellowship group of your choice

III. **Rest**
    A. Mind - Get six to eight hours of sleep nightly
    B. Body - Take naps as you need them and eat
       healthy snacks.
    C. Spirit - Schedule in re·creation time. Successful
       people make time for their inner selves.

If you notice the diagram below looks like a peace symbol, then you understand my point. Being well means being at peace with yourself. Take care of your temple. Your spirit lives there! "Life will always be," wrote Samuel Smiles, "to a large extent what we ourselves make it." Make your life a healthy one. Ride the cycle of life. Be well!

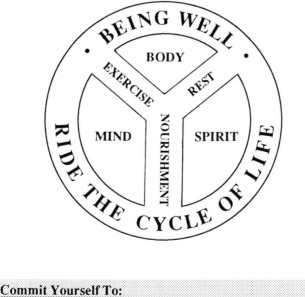

Commit Yourself To:
- Exercise
- Nourish   **YOURSELF**
- Rest

Lesson 21

ETHICS

Becoming A Person Of Character And Integrity

"No legacy is so rich as honesty."   William Shakespeare

You are now facing or will soon confront some of the most difficult decisions of your life. How do I tell my parent(s) that I am going to live for myself? Choose my own major? Make my own way? What do I do about the faculty member who doesn't seem to care about teaching me? My best friend is cheating...should I say anything? What about the honor code? My roommate is a problem drinker...maybe I am. What should I do? What do I want to do with my life?

It would be wonderful if I could give you ready-wrapped answers-to-go for these and all other ethical dilemmas you will face. It has been my experience though that simple solutions often do not fit complex problems. I know you will make up your own mind. Let me provide you with a decision making framework that has helped me. Maybe it will help you make good and informed decisions about your life.

We can impact the world positively by making good decisions that "give life" to situations and people rather than "take life away." You can live well and prosper by

57

looking out for your neighbor's well-being as well as your own.

Professor J. Wesley Robb of the University of Southern California taught me the following;

> *Before you act, think four thoughts:*
> 1. What is my motive in doing this act? What is my intention?
> 2. What is the applicable law or university policy?
> 3. What are the possible consequences of my actions?
> 4. What are my moral principles regarding this action?

Becoming a person of character *and* integrity means narrowing the distance between what you say and what you do and increasing the amount you care for yourself and for others.

This is a challenging task. It will be more attainable if you make ethical decisions, and learn from your mistakes when you do not. Kay Lyons proposes, "Yesterday is a cancelled check; tomorrow is a promissory note; today is the only cash you have — so spend it wisely." Making ethical decisions today will make your tomorrows more enjoyable and your yesterdays less regrettable. Take time to think before you act.

Commit Yourself To:
- Think, Feel
- Hope, Love, And Then...
- Act

HATE

Beware The Rhetoric Of Hate, It Will Consume You

> _"They first came for the communists and I didn't speak up, because I wasn't a communist. Then they came for the Jews and I didn't speak up, because I wasn't a Jew. Then they came for trade unionists and I didn't speak up, because I wasn't a trade unionist. Then they came for the Catholics and I didn't speak up, because I wasn't Catholic. Then they came for me and by that time there was no one left to speak up."_ Pastor Martin Niemoeller, Nazi victim

Beware, too, the violent behavior of hate. "The hardest thing," said one African-American student, "is reading the horrible things written about me in bathrooms." Acts of violence, hostile graffiti, and verbal abuse are becoming the daily staple for ethnic students on college and university campuses. Bigotry, racism, homophobia, and higher education would seem to be strange bedfellows. One would associate higher education with open mindedness and tolerance, yet inconceivable acts of hate by students crowd newsprint headlines.

"This naked display of racism is only one example of a general breakdown of civility on U.S. campuses...The 'idyllic vision' of college life often masks disturbing realities, including racism, sexism, homophobia, and anti-semitism," Times Magazine, May 1, 1990.

What can you do? First, do not speak the rhetoric of hate. This is, after all, America. We have extended an invitation to "the poor, huddled masses" and they have come calling, hopefully seeking " life, liberty, and the pursuit of happiness." To rob someone of this pursuit based on skin color, ethnicity, or sexual orientation is illegal, un-American, and worse, unethical. Widen your perspective by being a friend to all who would be your friend.

Second, remember that if we are picking or not picking on and abusing African Americans, Jews, Asians, Gays or The-Group-Of-The-Week, your group may be next. None of us will be truly free until all of us are free. Free to be ourselves, away from the darkness and life-sapping grip of racism, sexism, and other forms of hatred.

President Jimmy Carter once said, "Full participation by citizens of every race and ethnic origin in all aspects of American life, and particularly education, is essential to the growth and well-being of the nation." Rise to the occasion. *The letter "P" is the first letter of both patriotism and pluralism. It is also the first letter of the word perspective.* I propose to you as a leader and contributor to the new world order that we need a new perspective on patriotism that calls forth an acceptance of pluralism and tolerance from all of us. No one owns the truth. We are citizens of the world, as well as of our nations. We must live interdependently in peace. Hate destroys the hater and the hated.

The "fundamental fact" of being American is that this is a great nation which has special resources, opportunities, and responsibilities in the world made up of peoples from many other great nations. Freedom and Respect must regulate our affairs with one another. We must hang a sign on the door that says, "Hatred Hath No Place Here!"

Eleanor Roosevelt said, "Remember, no one can make you feel inferior without your consent." America in the twenty-first century can either be a beautiful mosaic of peace and justice for all or a nation broken and embittered by prejudice and hatred. It is our choice. Let us all work together to take the high road to life, liberty, and the pursuit of happiness.

To Honor Yourself, Your Family, Your Friends, Your Nation, and Your World.
- Beware The Rhetoric Of Hate. It Will Consume You.
- Love Yourself And Your Fellow Human Beings
- Create A Mosaic By Speaking The Language Of Friendship And Love.

SPIRITUALITY

You Do Not Have To Be "Religious" To Be Spiritual: Listen To The "Voice Within"

"I have ever thought religion a concern purely between our God and our consciences, for which we were accountable to Him, and not the priests. I have never told my own religion, nor scrutinized that of another. I never attempted to make a convert, nor wished to change anothers creed. I have ever judged of the religion of others by their lives...For it is in our lives, not from our words, that our religion must be read."   Thomas Jefferson

I believe that there is Spirit in the world and that the world is in Spirit. While the "voice within" me has called me to a specific manifestation of that Spirit, I believe that your voice may have called you to another place. The teachings of Jesus to _"love God and love your neighbor as you love yourself"_ have called me to be and do things in a different way than I likely would have done on my own. What teachings move and motivate you? Are you searching? Are you listening to the voice within?

It is ultimately important that you believe in something and I expect you to live fully according to your beliefs. It is my hope that you would associate yourself with a group of common believers and experience the Spirit in community.

Frankly, it does not matter to me what you believe in as long as it:

> A. Gives you hope
> B. Brings out the best in you
> C. Helps you be tolerant of others
> D. Contributes to your education
> E. Teaches you to love

Field or forest, synagogue, temple, mosque, church, or great hall, go to the place where you feel the Presence. Then, and only then, will you be whole and will your life be full. See, and feel, the spiritual nature of your existence. Know the blessing of being alive, with possibilities and potential waiting for your passionate attention.

And remember...in America we honor all expressions of spirituality. This at times causes us concern and uncomfortable feelings. You have a right, and a responsibility, I think, to believe what you will and act on your beliefs.

I believe what we see with our eyes is not all there is to see with our heart. What do you believe?

Seek:
• Your Deeper Self
• The Spirit In Simple Things
• Love And Tolerance Of Others

SENIORS

A Note To People In Transition

"Education is the ability to listen to almost anything without losing your temper or your self-confidence."
Robert Frost

As the information in the world doubles about every four years and nearly 8,000 scientific articles are published every day, it should be apparent by now that you do not know everything yet that you are going to need to know for a meaningful and productive personal and professional life.

So what? Here's what...

You are about to "start over" in the corporate, educational, legal, or grad school world. I hope you have learned to "love to learn." Einstein once had to look up his phone number to give it to a friend. Quizzed as to why the scientific genius didn't know his own number, Professor Einstein said, "I do not have to know it. I just have to know where to look it up."

Be patient when your employer or grad school professor treats you like the new kid on the block. *You are the new kid on the block.* New beginnings offer tremendous opportunities and demand a certain degree of humility. It is transition time again for you. Be patient, be poised, and keep your mind on the big picture. You are going to do fine!

It is, however, completely possible that you may not graduate right now. You may "stop out" for financial reasons, family matters, or other personal concerns. You can have a meaningful life, be a productive person, and for that matter be brilliant without a college degree. C.S. Lewis once observed that it was completely possible to be an M.A. and a fool! The degree will likely give you more options as your life progresses and I would encourage you to finish as soon as you can. With the degree or not, you are starting over, making a transition. Go slow, be humble, and allow yourself to glean from other's experiences. You will be wiser, happier, and better liked. Good Luck!

Say:
- I Am All Right. I Am Okay. I Am Going To Do Fine
- I Am New Here. I Will Figure It Out
- To Everything There Is A Season: This Is My Season To Start Over

HOMECOMING

Two Things For Parents To Think About

*"A child tells in the streets what its father and mother say
at home."*   The Talmud

There are a couple of things I believe parents should be told along with their students in new student orientation. Let's get these two items out on the table.

1. It takes many students longer than four years to complete a degree.

Increased degree requirements; computer education; an information explosion; and many other factors have driven universities and students to more courses, more sections, and more years. Be advised.

2. Many students will move back home after graduation.

Parents and students who take time to tally "start up" expenses find the numbers are frightening. The job search, relocation, apartment procurement, and associated expenses are costly proposals these days. It makes good sense in many cases to move home for awhile to save up for these expenses.

Also many students are taking longer and longer to find employment. The job market is volatile and world-wide competition is increasing. It may take a little more time to get started. Prepare for it. Your students may come home after graduation.

There are two things I would recommend students think about before moving back home for awhile:

1. You are returning to your parent's home. You are a visitor now. Be a good guest.

2. You have a right to be treated as a mature adult. You have the responsibility to act like one.

For better and for worse you are a family. Work at getting along with each other. It is never too late to make peace and learn to forgive. Now is the time to say, "thank you," and "I love you," or even, "I'll try."

Reflect:
- Parents: If your children want to come home after college it is an affirmation of your relationship.
- Students: If your parents will take you home this is a gift...be thankful.
- Parents and Students: Everyone cries about the breakup of the family...Why complain about spending more time together as family? Enjoy it...it is all too fleeting!

CONTRIBUTORSHIP

You Will Lead Occasionally, But You Can Always Contribute

"Great minds have purposes; others have wishes."
Washington Irving

Many books have been written and programs put together recently on the development of leadership, it's characteristics, relationships to success, and rewards. Dave Kovac and I believe a better and more realistic goal might be *contributorship.* In reality, few of us will lead the nation, a company or school board. We can, however, all make a contribution. By making daily contributions to our betterment, actualization of long term goals, or well-being of others, we prepare ourselves to become leaders when opportunities present themselves. There is no substitute for leadership by example. Setting the example we will call making a contribution.

Contributors are men and women of character who are open to the ideas of others. They search for better ways to do things, "never say never," and are teachable people who are willing to learn. Contributors are responsible and imaginative and work for the betterment of all concerned. They utilize existing resources and solicit new

69

ones. Contributors treat other people as they would like to be treated and "own their own evaluations" of others. They are respected because they respect others and are good stewards of themselves and their organizations. Contributors develop a good sense of humor and laugh with others, not at them. They are men and women of integrity who say what they mean and do what they say. Contributors admit mistakes and are patient with themselves and others.

President John F. Kennedy once said, "Ask not what your country can do for you. Ask what you can do for your country." Resolve yourself to be a contributor in each situation in which you are involved. Lead when called upon to serve; contribute each and every day. You will be making your campus, community, nation, and world a better place!

Choose:
- To Contribute Daily To The Betterment Of Self, Others, Community, Nation, And World
- To Make Ready To Lead While Allowing Others To Do The Same...No One Leads All The Time!
- Choose To Be A Woman Or Man Of Character; A Contributor

SUCCESS

Do Your Best. Be Your Best Self.

"To be successful, the first thing to do is fall in love with your work."   Sister Mary Lauretta

Do you want to be successful? Do you want to leave a mark on the world? Do you wish to do great things? I do!

A couple of years ago a college administrator friend told me he had seen graffiti on his campus that said: "Success: live fast, die young, and leave a beautiful corpse." How sad! How shallow! So scary that the author might have been serious. May I offer you a different definition of the true meaning of success?

John Wooden taught me about the real meaning of success. His ten NCAA Basketball Championships and loving family attest to his success. Coach Wooden said:

"Success is the peace of mind that comes from knowing you did the best you were capable of doing; and you are the only one that will ever know that." Contrary to the old adage, you can fool all the people all the time. But you cannot fool yourself. You are the only one who will know if you are doing your best, giving your all, making a contribution. Therefore, you alone will know in your heart if you are a success. You are the only one who will ever know. Know thyself!

Abraham Lincoln said, "I do the very best I know how, the very best I can; and I mean to keep on doing so until the end." An addition from Anne Frank, "We all live with the objective of being happy; our lives are all different and yet the same." I do not believe you will ever be happy, and for that matter, ever be successful, until you know in your heart and soul that you did your very best. You gave it your best shot. "You are the only one," writes Coach Wooden, "that will ever know." Seek your peace of mind. Be a success!

To Be A Success:
- Do Your Best. Be Your Best Self
- Love A Lot, Forgive Much
- You Are The One You Have To Please And Live With: Seek Your Peace Of Mind.

WARRIORSHIP

Overcoming The Fear Of Yourself

"The key to Warriorship...is not being afraid of who you are. Ultimately, that is the definition of bravery: not being afraid of yourself." Chögyam Trungpa

I have recently been reading a delightful book entitled, Shambhala: The Sacred Path of the Warrior. Trungpa has analyzed the primary ailments of our time and has challenged us to become warriors.

Trungpa proposes, "When we are afraid of ourselves and afraid of the seeming threat the world presents, then we become extremely selfish! We want to build our little nests, our own cocoons, so that we can live by ourselves in a secure way." He continues, "We must try to think how we can help this world. If we don't help, nobody will...You can never just relax, because the whole world needs help."

The whole world does need help and we must become warriors waging war on fear, and greed, and selfishness because the great majority of our societal ailments are born ot insecurity nurtured by fear of self.

Ultimately our success as individuals and as a species will be determined by the path we choose. The path of fear or the path of the warrior. The brave will choose to overcome fear and help the world.

Seek:
- The Sacred Path Of The Warrior
- To Help The World
- To Overcome Your Fear Of Yourself And Learn To Love And Accept Yourself

LOVE

All You Need Is Love

"Where there is love there is life."   Mohandas Gandhi

As I have watched my two daughters grow, I have realized that all I need is love. Some food sure. A little cash for goods and services. I live under a fifty-three year old cedar roof. But love is what I need. Og Mandino states, "Treasure the love you receive above all. It will survive long after your gold and good health have vanished." I treasure the love I have received.

Some of what I have written in this book was simplistic to you I'm sure. Some confusing. But hear this: It's **Love**. What is the meaning of Life? **Love**. What is the greatest thing? **Love**. What makes sex fantastic and children a blessing? **Love**. And what do I want you to do? That's right, **Love**! King's X says, "It's love, that keeps it all together. I just had to let you know. It's love."

With it, you have everything, without it, you are nothing. Your BMW will not console you when your parents die, nor will your savings account hold your hand when you suffer. But love will get you through because it always comes dressed as another person, as spiritual feelings, or an insight into self.

My book says, "love others as you love yourself." Do you love yourself? I cannot make it alone, and I don't think you can either. Together, in love, we could. You need to be loved and so do I. We will be loved as soon as we love ourselves and allow ourselves to be loved by others. We will have to forgive ourselves, let go of mistakes, and turn loose grudges against others. Leo Buscaglia advises, "Love is life...And if you miss love, you miss life."

Foreigner wrote, "I wanna know about love. I know you can show me." Let your love go, let it warm your friends, your self, your world. St. Paul said, "If I speak with the tongues of angels but do not have love, I am nothing." Let love be your way.

Please:
- Love God, Or That Which You Believe To Be Spirit
- Love Your Self: You Are Worthy!
- Love Your Neighbors: They Need It!

FEAR

The Great Immobilizer

"Avoiding danger is no safer in the long run than outright exposure. The fearful are caught as often as the bold."
Helen Keller

I have encountered many students who seem to be immobilized by fear. Fear of disappointing their parents, fear of not reaching their goals, fear of an uncertain future in a changing world dynamic. Most of all these students are afraid to fail.

"Don't be afraid to fail," writes H. Stanley Judd. "Don't waste energy trying to cover up failure. Learn from your failures and go on to the next challenge. IT'S OKAY TO FAIL. If you're not failing, you're not growing." This is good advice. Failure is just a temporary pause on the way to your success. It only lasts as long as we allow ourselves to be fixated on it. We must find the courage to get up, dust ourselves off, and go on.

Courage comes from within and demands that we remain faithful to our original intentions. Eddie Richen bacher wrote, "Courage is doing what you're afraid to do. There can be no courage unless you're scared." Life is sometimes scary for everyone!

Fear, the fear of failure, and being scared are all real emotions and part of being human. What we do with these feelings is what is important. I might suggest that you share your fears with a trusted friend, a resident assistant, your academic advisor, or a counselor. Sometimes the only way to get some sleep is to look under the bed and confront the "imagined horribles" that you see lurking in your fearful fantasy. Most of the time there is nothing there but your fear. Don't let this unwanted and unproductive emotion defeat you. Face it and it will shrink with the light of your self understanding. Face yourself and your future with hope, not fear!

Face The Facts:
• Fear Is A Normal Human Emotion
• Everyone Is Fearful At Some Time
• What We Do With Fear Is The Important Thing

LONELINESS

An Epidemic Sadness

"The loneliness of poor people in this country is so stark because of the absence of family and support networks. There is a total abandonment of the elderly and the homeless, in many cases even children. And it's incredible. I think in many parts of this country we're pioneering new levels of inhumanity." Jerry Brown, Former Governor, State of California

I would add students to Governor Brown's list of the lonely. Many students come to campus without functional family support or networks in place to provide a safety net when problems occur and loneliness sets upon them.

Huge research-focused universities do not appear to me to be places of warmth and welcome for many undergraduates. It is easy to feel like a social security number rather than a vibrant, valuable, and important human being.

I want to encourage you to "pioneer new levels of connectedness." It is difficult to reach out, but you must do it! Martin Buber said, "The fundamental fact of human existence is person with person." We need to be with others to be, to grow, to feel needed and wanted.

Some suggestions to combat loneliness and establish a network of associates and friends include:

- Live in a Residence Hall. Most halls have professional and paraprofessional staff who can assist you in adjusting to life on your own. Talk to your R.A. or Resident Director.

- Consult with the Director of Student Activities or Student Life regarding participation in university clubs, intramurals, or interest groups.

- Many academic departments will have "majors" groups where students meet with faculty for discussion and dialogue as well as social events.

- Professional counselors are available on or near every campus that I am aware of and they are prepared to assist you in a variety of problem resolution areas.

Just Do It. That is, get yourself up and out on campus. The joy of being connected with the lives of others will overcome the awkwardness of reaching out. Lao-Tzu said, "The journey of a thousand miles begins beneath your feet." Take the first step and let the journey begin.

George Bernard Shaw proposed, "The people who get on in this world are the people who get up and look for the circumstances they want, and if they can't find them, make them." Think about the circumstances you desire in order to overcome your loneliness and then get up and start moving in that direction. You will be glad you did!

Consider:
- Everyone I Know Feels Lonely Occasionally. This Is A Normal Human Condition, Like Fear
- Loneliness Can Be Overcome
- By Participating And Living Fully, You Will Be Helping Others As Well As Yourself

HAPPINESS

The Secret Of Happiness

"The greater part of our happiness or misery depends on our disposition and not on our circumstances."
Martha Washington

I believe that the secret of happiness is to learn to accept yourself as you are and then to take responsibility for your life. Happiness demands that you love yourself, share this love with others, and understand that your life is the result of your choices and your attitude about the things that happen to you. I believe a happy person is a loving person who has made peace with God or that which he or she believes to be Spirit. Being happy means being actively involved in the "Three F's":

> Family
> Friends
> Faith

I am painfully aware that some of you do not have the experience of a loving family, healthy and well friends, or a deep and abiding faith. Could this be at the root of your unhappiness? I believe it would be in your best interest to work today toward making peace with your family, establish relationships with friends who help you be your best self, and begin or continue your spiritual journey.

Olympic Gold Medalist Billy Mills states: "Happiness should be your personal goal. It should transcend all other goals you have in your life. If you are happy your life is improved in every way. It's the most powerful form of positive thinking. With it, all your goals can be realized." You must strive to be happy. You must desire and choose to be your best self. You may have to solicit the help of a friend or parent, or the professional experience of a teacher or counselor. Happiness is an emotion we can choose to experience daily, even hourly.

Walt Disney wrote, "All of our dreams can come true if we have the courage to pursue them." I believe you can find the courage to pursue your dreams inside your heart. Dare to dream. Dare to be great. Dare to make a contribution to the betterment of the world. Begin to live each day fully so that your life becomes a masterpiece.

Being happy means being yourself and learning to love yourself, then others. I have told you everything I know. These are my lessons, my hopes for you and me. Now it is your turn, your moment to create your life of love. Go with love, walk with the Spirit, and be happy!

In Love And Happiness Know:
- Happiness Is A Feeling We Can Choose
- Happiness Is A Worthy Goal
- The Secret Of Happiness Is Love!

A PARTING
THOUGHT

Or Two...

"If you want to solve the world's problems, you have to put your own household, your own individual life, in order first" Chögyam Trungpa

Surely the lessons of your life will come to you differently than my lessons have come to me. This is both natural and good. Natural, because we are unique individuals, similar in many ways yet different in subtler less known ways. Good, because life would be so indescribably boring if all that was known to one person could be instantly known as experiences by the other. Variety is one of the many spices of life. Yet, we share so much in common.

Secondly, it is both exhilarating and humbling that nearly everything I know can be put into a book this small. I have done my best for you and surely it will be too long there, too short here, and incomplete at best. But I have tried to help you, to "help the world." I promise to try and live more closely to my lessons as well. We are but human beings here so briefly, riddled with inconsistencies. Isn't it wonderful, amazing, and graceful that anyone loves us? Will Campbell said, "We're all bastards, but God loves us anyway." How powerful and life changing is Love!

Love never ends. While Thoreau said, "Most men live lives of quiet desperation," we do not have to live our lives this way. Let our lives be marked by passion, love, character, hope and patience. "We shall," the spiritual implores, "overcome. We shall overcome." We shall overcome our fear of ourselves and learn to live together in peace. We will learn to love, to jump into the arena of life.

We shall not say goodbye, but before we pause, hear Theodore Roosevelt:

> *"The credit in life does not go to the critic who stands on the sideline and points out where the strong stumble, but rather, the real credit in life goes to the man who is actually in the arena, whose face may get marred by sweat and dust, who knows great enthusiasm and great devotion and learns to spend himself in a worthy cause, who, at best if he wins, knows the thrill of high achievement and if he fails, at least fails while daring greatly, so that in his life his place will never be with those very cold and timid souls who know neither victory nor defeat."*

Enter the arena of life my friend!

With love,

Will Keim, Ph.D.